No Ocean Here

Stories in Verse about Women from Asia, Africa, and the Middle East

By Sweta Srivastava Vikram

Foreword by Marjorie McKinnon

From the World Voices Series

M o d e r n   H i s t o r y   P r e s s

From the World Voices Series

Distributed by Ingram Book Group, Bertram's Books (UK), Hachette Livre (France).

ISBN-13: 978-1-61599-157-0 Paperback
ISBN-13: 978-1-61599-191-4 Hardcover
ISBN-13: 978-1-61599-192-1 eBook

Published by Modern History Press
www.ModernHistoryPress.com

an Imprint of Loving Healing Press
5145 Pontiac Trail
Ann Arbor, MI 48105
www.LHPress.com
info@LHPress.com

Tollfree USA/CAN: 888-761-6268
London, England: 44-20-331-81304
FAX: 734-663-6861

Praise for the Poetry of Sweta Srivastava Vikram

"Vikram's wordsmithing is outstanding. I have read much poetry and have never seen such creativeness as that of this author. She allows her words to flow with rhythm and deepness. The wisdom that comes through her is beyond any I've seen."
—Irene Watson, *Reader Views*

"In *Kaleidoscope: An Asian Journey of Colors*, Sweta Srivastava Vikram re-appropriates color. Cultures and mythologies collide along the way, and the result is a chapbook that feels like a quest. In the end, the colors are a map to identity. The child's pink tonsils or the bride's red sari are not symbols, but rather mile markers. Like Vikram's poems, they lead toward understanding."
—Erica Wright, Senior Poetry Editor, *Guernica*

"This slim chapbook is a quick bite. Poems appear and disappear in the blink of an eye, but linger in consciousness longer than you might think they would. The use of colors is fascinating to the desi mind; we, as one poem remarks, 'exist in a hue of experiences.'"
—Vidya Pradhan, Editor, *India Currents*

"This chapbook is the dazzling display of a poet who teases us with fresh imagery and delicate linguistic craftsmanship. The real joy of this collection is its potential to be read in a single sitting, multiple times, with each subsequent reading revealing new insights. For poetry virgins, this text demands no sophisticated knowledge of poetics and literary discourse. To put simply, it is an accessible piece of enjoyable writing."
—Orchid Tierney, Editor, *Rem Magazine*, New Zealand

"I dove into this book of poems quickly and eagerly, then slowed down to savor the words and the images, marveling over Sweta Srivastava Vikram's unique mix of grace, humor, and eloquence, which forms a medley of beauty and color."
—Susan Ortlieb, *Suko's Notebook*

"Sweta has woven such a spell with her word usage and the symbolisms that the most complex becomes the simplest of all."
—Smita Singh, *VAANI*, UK

"I'm glad I found a new South Asian author, and will be following Vikram's work closely in the future."
—Swapna Krishna

"Sweta Srivastava Vikram's *Because All Is Not Lost: Verse On Grief* shares her personal loss and, in return, comforts the reader. Her beautifully crafted poems take the reader on a voyage that has to be undertaken by each of us individually."
—Patricia Carragon, *Brownstone Poets*

"....there is a bit of defiance in her words as the color beige takes over in old age and she fights to remain red, youthful. Overall, *Kaleidoscope: An Asian Journey of Colors* is an even stronger chapbook poetry collection than Because All Is Not Lost because it deals more than with just emotion and healing. Sweta Srivastava Vikram is a gifted poet..."
—Serena, *Savvy Verse and Wit*

"This is a collection populated by a recognizable but richly diverse and dramatic cast of family characters."
—Mary-Jane Newton, *Cha: An Asian Literary Journal*

"Sweta's poetic voice flows like water smoothing and shaping stones. With great skill she uncovers, sometimes tenderly and other times more forcefully, the shroud of fog surrounding the feminine archetype... she has created and nurtured a garden, a wordscape, in which trust and healing can flourish."
—Nick Purdon, author *The Road-shaped Heart*

"Sweta Srivastava Vikram holds her work close. Fold it one way, a poem of loss appears. Fold it yet again for a poem of longing. Her work is as structurally sound as the elements. It soars with anticipation. Vikram reveals lovely and powerful poems that will long linger."
—Doug Mathewson, Editor, *Blink-Ink*

Also by Sweta Srivastava Vikram

Poetry
Because All Is Not Lost
Kaleidoscope: An Asian Journey of Colors
Whispering Woes of Ganges & Zambezi
Not All Birds Sing
Beyond the Scent of Sorrow

Fiction
Perfectly Untraditional

Nonfiction
Mouth full: A collection of personal essays and poetry

For Papa, my father, and Anudit, my husband—my strength, support, and courage.

Contents

Foreword by Marjorie McKinnon

No Ocean Here presents poignant, passionate, perceptible portrait of girls and women in the developing countries of Asia, Africa, and the Middle East. It's a collection of poems that covers a myriad of subjects centered on social evils, such as domestic violence, honor killing, female infanticide, arranged marriage, bigotry, female excision, prostitution of widowhood, misuse of religion, child abuse and others. Most of the poems are either representative of interviews conducted by the poet Sweta Srivastava Vikram or inspired by true stories.

Despite being brought up in a safe, nurturing environment herself, Sweta brings an intrepid, confident voice to her poems. Her words reveal the harshness in the world with utmost beauty. The collection will haunt you. The book will strike a universal chord with audiences globally.

Since my space in this foreword is limited, I will speak only about childhood abuse, a subject especially relevant to my own life, and how this work touched my soul. When I was a child of thirteen, my father came into my bedroom as I slept on the bottom bunk, a rosary under my pillow and stole my life. In one ripping moment he destroyed my innocence. To cushion the agony of his nightmare visits I raced barefoot out to Rae Creek, half a mile from town, as often as I could. There I crossed the dusty road, climbed beneath the fence and moved like a shadow till I found my oak tree. I climbed the trunk and nestled my anorexic body in the curve of the branches. With pen and ink I wrote verse after verse, the only safe place I knew where I could hide my anguish. I saved all those poems until I entered recovery. By then there were many poems, all of them clearly defining what I had gone through and the stages of growth that spurted like a miracle despite the heavy hand of patriarchy that ruled my family. Those poems saved my life. It astonishes me how well Sweta understands the psychological state of victims. With utmost sensitivity, she uses words as a sword to fight back with, phrases that bring bravery, and insights that painted pictures as no artist's brush could.

No Ocean Here showed me a world of malice and ignorance in a way I had never seen before. Sweta's words have wings as they move you through the malevolence of life, sifting through all the bad moments of not only the society she writes about, but also of her gender. She fearlessly creates from the depth of her soul. And you weep when you read lines like "rarely heard, she is/just an asterisk on an endless list.*"

Sweta's poems have magic. She speaks for all the girls who have been ravished, whose virtue has been plundered. She raises her voice for all the women who continue to live with the insanity. Despite our worlds being oceans apart, when I read her poems, I shifted painfully into the world of inner grief she brings forth. I understand all that she understands; I feel all that she feels.

In her poem, "Mayit Nar", she writes about an abuse too painful to consider and yet in the last stanza she finds unblemished spirituality when she writes:

> Her palms, reaching out to God
> hold onto the hem of ambiguity
> wishing the silence of the ocean
> would explain the mirage of her freedom.

Using words as if they were candles lighting her way, Sweta beckons you, guides you, at times cushioning the blows with her insights, with the beauty of her metaphors. You find yourself in awe at her ability to dispassionately remove herself from the prison that she writes about. In "So They Can Be Cured", she says in the third stanza:

> A crooked stick won't make her straight.
> A rape can't *correct* her—
> you *correct* what's wrong.

Sweta gives voice to all that needs to be heard even as she chooses phrases that dance upon your tongue such as "Bids adieu to her abducted existence."

Marjorie McKinnon is the Founder of the Lamplighter Movement and author of *Repair Your Life: A Program for Recovery from Incest & Childhood Sexual Abuse.*

Introduction

Living in New York has its many advantages, one of which is the ability to observe and interact with people from different ethnicities and races. And in the process, eventually, learn about the rights, roles, and conditions of women in their respective cultures.

Over a period of time, every story I heard, every interview I conducted led me to believe that women and girls in many parts of the world, even today, deal with gender inequality and violence. Numerous issues still exist in all areas of life, ranging from the cultural, political to economic. Reports by non-profit organizations confirm that women often are stripped of basic human rights in developing and under-developed countries. They start life without adequate means of nutrition, learning, and protection.

Domestic violence, illiteracy, death in childbirth, female infanticide, poor healthcare, rape, trafficking, torture, child abuse, acid throwing, gender bias, bride burning, and illiteracy are just some of the crimes that continue to prevail in societies and impact all socio-economic groups. Unfortunately, while education, politics, media, and culture play an important role they don't necessarily empower women.

The atrocities don't suggest that men are the sole villains. In many instances, women are the perpetrators—harboring killers, encouraging bride burning and wife beating, conducting female excision and breast-ironing or even killing their daughters to maintain their family's honor.

No Ocean Here chronicles palpable stories of women and girls, told through poems, in certain parts of Asia, Africa, and the Middle East. The poems, inspired by true stories or personal interviews, bear testimony and reveal the harsh realities impacting the lives of women.

I decided to write this book because listening, telling, and writing the stories of those who can't write them will create awareness. I am honored to be able to give victims a voice and survivors a chance. I can only pray that the book urges readers to empathize, and help. If it can influence one person to go home and hug his wife and daughter, I would consider myself blessed. If it can inspire one woman to stop being a perpetrator, I would feel fortunate. If the book can provide even a handful of women, in unfortunate situations, strength and courage to say NO, I would be humbled. As Helen Keller said, "Avoiding danger is no safer in the long run than outright exposure. The fearful are caught as often as the bold."

Acknowledgements

No Ocean Here took me to places, physically and emotionally, I can't even begin to describe—some days were traumatic, some were bleary, few were hopeful. There are many people whose contribution I'd like to acknowledge because they made the book happen.

I'd like to express my gratitude to my friend and fellow poet, Abby Adams, for her insight, patience, and forthrightness. She is the best reader one could ask for. A special thanks to Hadeel Assali, Ernest Dempsey, Sugi Ganeshananthan, Rabea Murtaza, Norma Liliana Valdez, and Vijaya Vavilikolanu for their invaluable input. The women who confided their darkest fears and cultural, familial secrets to me and would rather go unnamed, I salute you. Your courage inspires me.

I would like to thank Justen Ahren, West Tisbury Poet Laureate and Director of the Martha's Vineyard Writers Residency, for his hospitality and support. It was at his residency when I conceived the idea for my book. Special thanks to my fellow poets and writers at Martha's Vineyard Writers Residency for their encouragement. At the Colrain Poetry Manuscript Conference, I'd like to express my gratitude to conference founder Joan Houlihan, Martha Rhodes (Four Way Books), and Fred Marchant (Professor, Department of English Director, and director of Creative Writing and The *Poetry* Center, Suffolk University). I'd also like to acknowledge the writers and artists-in-residence at Colrain for their comments.

I am grateful for my family's encouragement, especially my father who taught me that doing the right thing and becoming a good human being was far more important than earning high grades or a big paycheck. Much gratitude to the undying support of all my friends, especially Jaya Sharan and Rashi Singhvi Baid. I couldn't have stayed sane through the research process had it not been for the two of them. Thanks to my husband, Anudit, for always being there—be it for brainstorming the cover or wiping my tears every time I heard a story, or for patiently pulling me out of those dark moments where activist poetry can drown a poet. I want to thank my nieces, Diya and Sana, who enthusiastically encourage me to write every day. I pray the world is a better place by the time they grow up.

My immense gratitude to my editor, Sherry Quan Lee, for her eloquence, empathy, and vision. Her advice made the manuscript so much stronger. And finally, I thank Victor R. Volkman at Modern History Press for taking risks and continuing to believe in my work. I cherish working with him.

"I do not wish [women] to have power over men;
but over themselves."
~ Mary Wollstonecraft

No Ocean Here

She is the seed inside an olive
set in a porcelain white bowl.
After the vultures chew her sheath,
she is forsaken to be buried whole.

I awaken in a cruel world—

no ocean here

even with the balm of poetry
so I am told.

Like a gypsy with no shoes,
I walk humbly through cultures,
documenting stories

for women without a voice.

She Is Story

The ants in the wall
don't know her.

The roaches breeding
on the leftovers disregard her.

The house lizard mocks
her inability to detach.

The tides in the ocean
urge her to tell her story.

There Is Something Wrong with the World

When women who are compelled to kill their own youth
become invisible like soot inside chimneys.

When the only math a girl knows
is to count the dead babies in her arms.

When the only science she understands
is that her womb is a pomegranate with seeds.

When the only respect she seeks
is going to bed without handprints on her face.

Her Wounds Are Mysterious

She wasn't always a fallen leaf,
she danced.

Pursuing the tartness of Indian
summer upside down, swinging
from the branch of a tree,
her legs tapped the breeze
on grandma's porch.

Now, like the Saharan desert
hiding imprints etched by callous passersby,
she is older and forlorn.

Her wounds are mysterious
like the Congo; the depth unseen
to the world but home to insects
rarely heard, she is
just an asterisk on an endless list*

Nameless Face

The rituals of purdah may vary with differing religions, cultures, and locations, but in traditional Islamic and Hindu culture, women are only allowed to communicate with "outsiders" by confining themselves to a screen by way of a veil.

Dogma,
ancient like tombs in Egypt,
makes her a prisoner burning—
a nameless face with no features.

At least mummification preserves
the soul and spirit of those dead;

compulsorily covering of flesh and blood
kills the butterfly, the cocoon weeps.

She is patient. She tries to reason
but his tongue is dirty, his heart numb.

Honor Killing

It's been estimated that over 20,000 women in the Middle East and Southwest Asia, where Islam is practiced, are killed by their family members if the latter thinks the victim has brought disgrace to the family or community.

Dead, she stares at the sea
as it carries her bones
thrown by guards,
smoking water pipes.

Her mother's mouth fills with sand,
her father and brothers' hands are covered
with gloves to cleanse the stains
left on the walls of their family
by a man who spread her legs,
tore her apart like a coyote.

Right before her murder, she didn't see
the silhouette of her face
in her grandmother's heart.

Apparently the family's pride lies
underneath her skirt,
in the space between her legs.

Mayit Nar

In some parts of Gaza, mayit nar (acid) is thrown on women who
don't cover their faces.

When she doesn't smother her skin
with moods of political changes,
he hurls *mayit nar* to burn it,
her body turns cold with fire and water.

When she wears a mask
of crumpled sheets on her desires,
he paints pictures of her warm, naked body
with brushes of sin inside his head.

Her palms, reaching out to God
hold onto the hem of ambiguity
wishing the silence of the ocean
would explain the mirage of her freedom.

To Test Her Character

In some countries, most recently in Egypt, a virginity test is conducted to determine whether a girl has been raped.

Even the moon bleeds
when the doctor inserts a finger
inside the victim
to test her character,
verify if she was *worth* the complaint.

The tip of the boat tilts
with the weight of grief.

She awakens to a new world
where theory is contaminated,
her dignity on trial.

The ripples in the river sink faith
like a block of cement,
the fishes nibble on her tragedy.

Labeled Immodest

Sharing Chelow kebab at a female Iranian professor's dinner table,
she also shared her story.

Accused that her clothes spread
adultery, orange jam on white bread,
when she protested for civil rights.

Footsteps of rape
followed her into prison,
stoning awaited her at every corner,
beatings covered her skin,
but the woman, she, was labeled *immodest.*

With sorrow in her eyes,
she gazed at the moonless sky,
"You can't kill someone
who already is dead."

So They Can Be Cured

In South Africa, to suppress lesbians, they are sometimes raped so they can be "cured" of their homosexuality.

She was born this way or maybe not,
but she holds no apology for who she is.

It seems that society has run short of excuses
to justify its mindless fear
and violence towards women.

A crooked stick won't make her straight.
A rape can't *correct* her—
you *correct* what's wrong.

She numbs the tip of her cords,
drinks
her tears,
and the abyss of pain mutes
the hurricane of crime.

Purdah

Purdah, a cultural tradition that keeps women concealed and separated from men and strangers, is practiced in Southeast Asia and the Middle East.

Ruksana is a caged bird, wings clipped—
wearing a veil over her smile
her lips can't touch autumn,
not the way she wants—
under the blue spread
without fences of remorse.

She wants to kiss
the tip of a rose bloom in a park,
not in the deserted verandah
of her room,
hidden behind curtains.

Skin wants to be teased
by the touch
of a breeze. Honeyed fingers long
to feel hues of orange, black, and white
in a butterfly's body, not the shades in the spice rack
displayed in her mother's *only* room.

Prophet Rumi said,
"But ignorant men dominate women."

She listens to his words and makes a wish
to be free.

War

In memory of women who became victims of war in Central Jaffna, Sri Lanka.

The sun was shining on shells
of burnt-out houses in their neighborhood.
Her mother, sister, and she were drinking

coffee, thanking bees for leaving them alone
when three men in uniforms entered

their house under the pretense of search.

All cavities of the women's trust were emptied out
when each man selected a victim:

her mother's body, stuffed inside soil,
was stomped by feet and questions,
her sister was dragged by her dark breasts,
and she was turned to debris and dust.

That was the last sunset
the three enjoyed as a family.
—the dead moved on,
those alive sleep with their eyes open.

Arranged Marriage

In many patriarchal societies, the men in a woman's life determine her worth.

The father who brought her up insisted
she breathes through windows of silence.

He promised her life to a bully
who plundered her temple every night.

She rubbed the swelling on her belly,
wondering if the baby too would endure her horror.

Virgin Goddess

Based on a ritual in Nepal where pre-pubescent, virgin girls are selected through rigorous process and worshipped as living goddesses.

She did not ask for any of the fuss—
for people to touch her dainty feet,
wash her toes with honey and milk
beg her hands to bless them.

It was all *their* decision.
They scrutinized her family's history,
made sure her mouth had twenty teeth,
her body and dreams virgin
like an angel.

She was human,
desiring to roll marbles
in her baby palms, hide her face
in the warmth of her mother's skin
hide under her crisp cotton *sari*

but, they turned her into stone
to be worshipped.

She was a child wanting to play
in the mud, the same brown soil
thrown in her face
when she outgrew their needs.

She was too young to understand why
when blood touched her thighs
of puberty, vulnerable yet strong like deer's,
the Goddess vacated her body.

Brothel

Every year, thousands of girls are trafficked from Nepal into India for commercial sex work. Most of these girls come from poor families, so they are lured by the promise of employment or marriage.

If young, feminine feet crossed the border,
poverty would abandon their families.
Paper, with Gandhi's face embossed, would live

in wallets, such are promises made by men
who dig tunnels of opportunity
through starved eyes.

Illiterate, poor fathers with blindfolds
should never be given a pen. But daughters aren't allowed
to say a word

not even when thumbprints seal
the fate of their adult years
and the promised destination turns to be a brothel.

An empty suitcase is given,
so they can bring back to Kathmandu
pieces of their experiences for their younger sisters.

How do they tell their story? Abused
sometimes 40 times a day, they don't blink,
just fill their bags with bricks for their parents' house.

Female Excision

Based on true stories of female excision victims in Africa.

She was playing hide-n-seek with her mother
and her aunts, so she hid behind the door.
Maybe it was an easy spot, or maybe not,
bad intentions can kidnap anywhere.

Palms wrapped her unsuspecting eyes,
a familiar voice said, "Ready or not, here I come!"
Banter bounced against the walls
and stifled her appeal for mercy.

A sharp, metallic object plundered her innocence
as a geyser of blood replaced her missing body part.
She was told the excision,
removal of her external female genitalia without anesthesia,
was for her good.

Breast Ironing

*In Cameroon, the process of "breast ironing" continues to scar
pubescent girls.*

One day, she dreams to have her own house
with walls the color of rainbow
where hammers heated over hot coal,
grinding stone, and mortar pestles will not
wage a war against her unsuspecting breasts—
behind closed doors.

She will finally have her own place
to grieve and return to life—
a haven where stories will have
different ends,
mothers won't massage
their daughters' developing chests,
destroying signs of emerging womanhood.

The petals of red bougainvillea will fill
the current of the winds.
Seated in a rocking chair,
her braid will sway back and forth.
Her shadow will finally not stare
at the blades of the ceiling fan,
waiting for the torture to end.

Child Abuse

Cases of child abuse and sexual exploitation, often gone unreported, continue to be on the rise in many parts of the developing world. Very often, the perpetrators are family members, teachers, and other primary care givers.

She was nestled against a pillow
when he entered
her mid-afternoon nap.

Her stomach twisted
when she saw the glint in his gold teeth.
He tickled her
with flowers of deceit,
nailed her to the bed.

She pleaded
with empty hands
betrayal in his eyes

what did I do wrong?

Nothing, his stares declared.

She can't pray,
her faith has become too dark.

Blasphemy

Often, low values are associated with female babies, especially in India and China.

Congratulatory words
—targeted at her mother's unfruitful egg—
hoped cholera would consume the baby girl,
like the flame of wrath swallows *ghee*

and another baby girl is consumed by antiquated customs,
mourning ceremonies accompanying her birth
because a female child is considered blasphemy.

And Another Girl

The preference for male children is deeply rooted in Asian society.

An invention in biogenetics, a PhD attributed to his name.
A bank account, fat like whale blubber,
helps grow his ego like cancer.

An apartment big enough to accommodate
his puerile intentions and the entire town
she abandoned to flap beneath his dreams.

But he complains

    A girl, after a girl, and another girl.

She breathes unspoken words
as the lavender in her heart wilts,
knowing the sex-determining letter is his.

Caretaker of Graves

Based on the ongoing issue of female infanticide.

The sun doesn't sink until 8 p.m.
but she sees darkness of bats all day.

Tidal waves of melancholy mix
with seeds plowed in her every year.

Mouth filled with muffled cries,
hospitals and conspirators in doctors' clothes
shadow her throughout married life.

Frogs get used to the air at night
but her murdered womb mourns scars.

Girls Are Like Leeches, Grandma Says

In South Asia, a male child is often preferred because he is expected to take care of the parents in their old age. But theory and reality are not always in sync.

Girls are a mistake, grandma blurted.
as she crocheted complications into her traditional ways.
Her words, bitterer than *Neem.*

Why do you say that?
Her granddaughter asked.

Girls are like leeches, carrying parasites
in their gut, drinking blood of people in their lives.
But you can depend on boys in old age!

The absurdity of her theory made her granddaughter ask
so why do you live with my mom
when you have a son to take care of you?

Ode to My Aunt

She died in childbirth, after having been put through multiple pregnancies, despite her congenital heart condition.

I.

The walls of her house
do not hold any scent of her.
Holes have been cemented
with new relationships.

But I have seen glimpses of her
behind my father's thick glasses.
A man who seldom cries,
yet the brother in him sheds a tear
when the ghost of his sister
haunts him.

On my recent trip to India,
Father handed me my aunt's journal—

although I never met her,
her prayers whispered to me.

II.

I wish you had run away
even when your belly, stuffed,
like spicy bitter gourd,
had you at the corner of fear and guilt.

Did you have the chance? Not once,
not twice but four times?

Warnings
obvious like rains in July
knocked. Yet, my aunt's tiny bones
fused with the hole in her heart.

Her smile hidden
as she ran backwards,
all five feet three inches of her
knowing what lay ahead.

Anything for a Son

Based on the story of a girl who was adopted after her mother died in childbirth. She grew up noticing that she was different from others in her family. Her birth mother, despite being sick, went through multiple pregnancies, out of choice, in the hope of having a male child.

Radha understood she was different
from her other siblings—
dressed by distant love
and maids who weren't her mother.

She heard tales
from her neighbors burning
incense, whispering to the almighty,
about the woman with a hole in her heart.

That was Shanti,
Radha's mother who,
at twenty-two, learned to wrap herself
in sheets of fertility, and loaned her body,
against her doctor's orders,
until, trying to fill her cradle with a boy
for the fourth time,
her story came to an end.

But Prayers Too Were Biased, Like Love

Estimates show that though most developing countries have made considerable progress in reducing the gender gap in school enrollment, many nations will not meet the education Millennium Development Goals (MDGs) by 2015.

Maya was told her family couldn't afford air,
so she smothered her aspirations,
needs vanquished as leaves in fall.

Maya's brothers dawdled away the hours with marbles at school
while she chased the fragrance of learning
hoping the ink would leak into her pores
and heal the abscesses on her bare feet.

A victim of the societal guillotine,
she cries until the night envelops her
with the only fine print she recognizes:
A woman, a sty in the eye.

Illiterate by Choice

*Based on a true story about a married man who felt belittled
because his wife could read and write, even though he chose to
remain illiterate.*

Childhood slithered
like a snake over sand.

All made choices—

she kicked hard,
studied on the sly under the banyan tree
while he, her future beau, spread his limbs
giving voice to his masculinity.

Years later, when she could read every letter
directed from the post office towards their house,
her husband felt threatened and ashamed

he wouldn't allow his wife
to read his personal notes, instead
he would go to a friend.

How could the wife feel sorry for the man
who'd rather see blisters on her hands from baking bread,
than to see her read and write?

Ocean of Knowledge

Though vital to sustainable development, studies show that education doesn't guarantee empowerment to women in the developing world. Socio-cultural factors play an important role.

Within the school of her girlfriends,
she was called *mermaid with fins of luck*.

Unlike her friends, she was permitted to *live*,
by her family in the ocean of knowledge,
soak her breasts
in the air singing to seagulls.
She entered places
where rocks weren't covered
with stench of garlic, onions, and curry powder.

But one year after her marriage,
obscenities dressed her husband's tongue.
A shark, he mauled her
night after night, drank her blood.
Her requests for respite faded in their empty house.

Fins don't let you walk,
she forgot.
She swam like a lost mermaid,
in circles,
unable to swim away.

Loud Woman No Good

Although women continue to be victimized in many instances, some have become perpetrators of domestic violence.

She is forced
to whisper every thought
that impregnates her brain.
loud woman, no good

She piles bodies
of opinion entering
the mouth of her house,
so the draft doesn't mock her.
loud woman, no good

She rubs sandalwood
on her forehead,
so the stain of accusations
doesn't announce itself.
loud woman, no good

She cries,
loud woman, no good

She whispers
loud woman, no good

How can she escape the smell
of burning wishes? Her life turned to ashes
by female perpetrators
who want the cycle of abuse
to never end.

A Good Woman

In South East Asia, women's roles and rights are often considered less important than their male counterparts.

She is tired of women—
mothers, aunts, cousins teaching
her what it means to be a *good woman.*

She is stripped
by poisoned arrows of judgment
peeling the skin of peach
while spitting the pit,
tearing her pride to shreds,
evaluating her suitability
as a carrier for seeds,
to serve a man's needs.

She is no scholar,
just a Phenomenal Woman*
who calls upon poetry
to describe her journey.

Phenomenal Woman, poem by Maya Angelou

A Business Deal

*Poverty leads many low-income families to marry their daughters to
older men with money.*

To her father, she was a business deal,
a dark song, not a daughter.

Ignoring the veins on her forehead,
he married her to false teeth and arthritis.

Her husband treated her like a whore.

How could she go to sleep
knowing incense wouldn't kill
the smell of betrayal?

She's saving her curses.

Skin Color

In several parts of India, Hindu women are subjected to traditional arranged marriages where their desirability is evaluated based on their skin color.

Every Monday, cream whitens her cheeks,
kohl disguises the crypt of her fears.

Braid, like a rat caught in a trap on the windowsill
ties a noose around her desires.

Red dot on her forehead decides
the direction of the next sixty years:

will she cross the window,
arrive safely at the gate of her dreams?
Or will she spend days
looking through it?

Suicide Note

In India, women have been known to commit suicide because their families couldn't provide adequate dowries.

Her father stands erect
his sun burnt face and limp arms tell her
there is no dowry;

she will never wear vermillion in her hair
she will never be surrounded
by silly jokes and beautiful flesh.

She is his first-born—
wiser than he knows.

Inhaling hunger,
she takes to the road,
knowing what needs to be done—
hoping it will buy her family peace.

Looking inside the house
where walls of struggles stand quietly,
she calls out to her sisters,
holds them tenderly
through their ill-fitting clothes,
one last time—

Before her father's head hangs in shame,
or his shirt becomes blood-stained—
she ends

          her life.

Mother-in-law

In many joint families in South Asia where two generations live together in the same house, the mother-in-law holds the reigns to the family. And often the son and other members follow her orders without debate.

He obeys his mother.
She manipulates the clock inside of him,
tells him the exact time

to paint his wife purple and blue.
The second and minutes direct the frequency
of cuts and slashes of verbal abuse.

Once he exits his mother's room,
he hangs his head
in shame.
Nicknames his action: *son's duty.*

When she, his wife, climbs steps
to reason with him—
he sketches drawings on her face
that darken the dawn.

Dowry Deaths

Many women in India are burnt to death (or driven to commit suicide) for not providing adequate dowry payments to their husbands and in-laws. Dowry deaths are one of the many types of violence against women in South Asia.

Seven rounds around *Agni*, the sacred fire,
hundreds of eyes, millions of hopes, heard
the promises made at their wedding ceremony:

*he would build fences so high
even the shadow of sorrow
couldn't trespass,
happiness would be tucked
in the folds of her sari.*

Warnings were everywhere:
the night hid the stars
leaves whispered secrets.
Death, death, death the parakeet screeched
for months, mocking her.

How did she miss the signs?

Whoever he is, he didn't hold up her *sari*
to touch her waist or kiss her neck.
Instead, creeping up behind his wife,
his icy bones grew greedy,
demanded more *dowry*.

Like a hermit she withdrew,
and the angry moans of *Agni*
moved towards her, engulfing
her faith and flesh whole.

Smell of Burnt Curry and Skin

Many women in Bangladesh have been victims of acid throwing attacks because they couldn't procure the amount of dowry their husbands and in-laws desired.

She was washing *Hilsa* fish, peeling
its scales when a thorn entered her fingers.
As she washed the blood from them,
blood rose in her husband's eyes.

The delay in dinner
brought up what had never been sealed—
his discontentment with the dowry
she'd brought when they got married.

It wasn't the first time
taunts, bitter like stale milk, filled the air.
It wasn't the first time
his temper spat like mustard seeds in hot oil.
It wasn't the first time
his hands marinated her body with beatings.
It wasn't the first time
he'd carefully avoided hitting her face.
It wasn't the first time
he swore to sell her to a man in Middle East.
It wasn't the first time
she refused to pimp her body, live with another man.

She wiped her tears,
mixed them into the onion and tomato paste.
He returned in a few seconds,
threw acid in her face, then disappeared like vapor.

The smell of burnt curry and skin,
are memories she takes with her everywhere.

Sex Slave, No Ocean Here

Studies show that women in developing countries often do not have sexual autonomy. Marital rapes go underreported because personal, cultural, and societal beliefs prevent a woman from reporting the assault.

Devour, masticate, and *spit*—
his favorite verbs drown the moon
of her desires. She cries
afraid of what wounds morning will flaunt
to branches of her tree.

He snickers,
masking the trail left behind by the demons
hidden inside his locket, hung
by chunks of gold. Running his hands
through her pride, he whispers,

There is no ocean here to listen to you.

The fog of expectation lifts from underneath her boat,
she becomes his sex slave every night.

Marriage Isn't a License to Rape

*Based on the life of a girl in Mumbai who has been putting up with
spousal rape for over a decade.*

Though years have passed, every night
he transforms into evil—
her breath fades.

She shuts her eyes
clasps her fingers,
and hopes no one enters the black waters
and sees the hole in her fiction story
recognizing she's not with the man
he had once promised to be.

He is someone she barely knows.

*No, this is no way
for a husband to treat his wife,
clean her up like bone in goat curry,*

she repeats to herself—sometimes
when she is too tired to want to die—

*marriage isn't a license to rape.
marriage isn't a license to rape.*

Heavier, Holding Her

Ceaseless is her pain:
like rocks picked, beaten
by the waves in the seas,
thrown beyond geographies;

A rope tugs a boat,
a rope chokes her neck.
Sadly, she doesn't want this long life
where the breeze becomes heavier
holding her.

Auto Immune Deficiency Syndrome

*According to AVERT, an international HIV and AIDS charity
based out of UK, nearly a third of the long-distance truckers in
India are carriers of the AIDS virus.*[1]

White sheets of satin bury
her desires forever as she roams

around her solitary room,
barefoot, with an infested

womb that might never see a baby,
red walls sunken where she once kept hopes hidden.

She had trusted the man,
who made sacred promises like religion. He spread

love, blackberry preserve on bread—
a disease at every stop his feet and truck made.

[1] Pandey, A et al (2008) *'Risk behaviour, sexually transmitted infections and HIV among long-distance truck drivers: a cross-sectional survey along national highways in India'*, AIDS 2008, 22(5): 81-90

HIV, Mother to Child

In low and middle-income countries, more than 90% of HIV cases are the result of mother-to-child transmission during pregnancy, labor and delivery, or breastfeeding.

This summer he would have been gone
for three full moons and their child's

arrival. As she awaits the beginning of the end
of the ruthless gift he gave them, separating

stories from his tongue into her body,
Mother Earth becomes her confidante.

Baby in her arms, she asks they be sung a lullaby.

Freedom

Widowhood is a burden women pay for heavily in developing countries.

I.

At twenty, the relatives brought her dark honey.
Minutes were inscribed,
her future sealed for what was,
her family thought, a good deal.

But no one chose to see
the unrest in her breath,
for forty years
her eyes talked to the rain.

At sixty, at her husband's wake,
she dug through the tunnel
of memories,

> *coerced to be a perpetual giver—*
> *a daughter, mother, and a wife*

sugar tasted bitter.

Now, she has found a best friend
in the solitude of freedom,

bids adieu
to her abducted existence.

II.

Like grains of rice in a sack,
coalesced, they can't stand alone
but can be tasted individually.

Ordered to enchant the males
in their galaxy, choice isn't their own.

They are ash.
Dead men moved on; widows are passed around.

III.

If he dies before her
She will be treated like a witch
burnt alive, or shared
with the village like a bag of compost.

And if she dies before her husband,
his tears will be rewarded
with brown cheeks, thighs, and young breasts.

Superwoman

Even in educated, modern families, men and women are not expected to do an equal share of housework despite both the husband and wife keeping jobs.

Her poems smell of onions,
even the raw air disapproves.

She is tired of being a superwoman—
slicing her dreams
for dinner, running
from wall to cement,
picking up pieces
of wishes not her own,
looking beautiful during the day,
abandoned by prayers at night.

She turns on the water in the sink,
it drowns the sound of her tears.
Sighing, she pounds her fists into bread dough
until the blue veins on her fingers squirm
and she blames the onions.

Listen

Women can tie a knot
of secrets—
stash it inside
their bras, braid it
from head to shoulder,
paint it onto their nails,
rub it into their blush
and mix it into a pot of broth,
serve it to their family for dinner.

Next time you eat soup,
listen
each morsel reveals a story.

Publishing Acknowledgements

"Listen" appeared in *The Tower Journal*, Vol. III, No. 2 (April 2009)

"Arranged Marriage" appeared in *The Electronic Monsoon Magazine* as "Is anything really mine?" (2011)

"She Is Story" appeared in *The Enchanting Verses Literary Review* under the title "Identity, Unknown" (March 2012)

"Auto Immune Deficiency Syndrome" appeared in *Bell Bajao* (October 2012)

"Skin Color" appeared in *Contemporary Literary Review India* as "Arranged Marriage" (December 2012)

"A Good Woman" appeared in *Global Fusion Voices* as "Who am I?"(January 2012)

"Female Excision" appeared in *Breadcrumb Scabs Magazine* as "Unfulfilled Desires."

"Caretaker of Graves" appeared in *Danse Macabre – An Online Literary Magazine* as "Killing, but not just a girl child."

"Blasphemy" appeared in *Danse Macabre – An Online Literary Magazine* as "I was nicknamed Sea of Curse."

"Dead conscience" appeared in *Bird's Eye reView: poetry from a different perspective* as "A Business Deal."

About the Author

Sweta Srivastava Vikram is an award-winning writer, two times Pushcart Prize nominated-poet, novelist, author, essayist, columnist, and educator whose musings have translated into four chapbooks of poetry, two collaborative collections of poetry, a novel, and a non-fiction book of prose and poems. Her work has appeared in several anthologies, literary journals, and online publications across six countries in three continents. A graduate of Columbia University, she reads her work, teaches creative writing workshops, and gives talks at universities and schools across the globe. Sweta lives in New York City with her husband.

Visit the author's website at www.swetavikram.com

Introducing the World Voices Series

This series highlights the best English-language autobiography, fiction, and poetry of diverse voices from Africa, Asia, the Caribbean, and South America.

Because All Is Not Lost: Verse on Grief
By Sweta Srivastava Vikram

Kaleidoscope: An Asian Journey with Colors.
By Sweta Srivastava Vikram

The Blue Fairy and other tales of transcendence
By Ernest Dempsey

Iraq Through a Bullet Hole: A Civilian Wikileaks
by Issam Jameel

The Road-Shaped Heart
by Nick Purdon

Beyond the Scent of Sorrow
By Sweta Srivastava Vikram

A Short History of the Short Story
By Gulnaz Fatma

No Ocean Here
by Sweta Srivastava Vikram

MODERN
HISTORY
PRESS

from Modern History Press
http://www.modernhistorypress.com/world-voices/

www.ingramcontent.com/pod-product-compliance
Lightning Source LLC
LaVergne TN
LVHW021135080426
835509LV00010B/1362